Parent Involvement Activities

7 Secrets to Effectively Bonding With Your Child for a Lifelong Healthy Parents and Children Relationship

Frank Dixon

Before we begin, I have something special waiting for you. An action-packed 1 page printout with a few quick & easy tips taken from this book that you can start using today to become a better parent right now!

It's my gift to you, free of cost. Think of it as my way of saying thank you to you for purchasing this book.

Claim your download of Profoundly Positive Parenting with Frank Dixon by scanning the QR code below and join my mailing list.

Sign up below to grab your free copy, print it out and hang it on the fridge!

Sign Up By Scanning The QR Code With Your Phone's Camera To Be Redirected To A Page To Enter Your Email And Receive INSTANT Access To Your Download

Before we jump in, I'd like to express my gratitude. I know this mustn't be the first book you came across and yet you still decided to give it a read. There are numerous courses and guides you could have picked instead that promise to make you an ideal and well-rounded parent while raising your children to be the best they can be.

But for some reason, mine stood out from the rest and this makes me the happiest person on the planet right now. If you stick with it, I promise this will be a worthwhile read.

In the pages that follow, you're going to learn the best parenting skills so that your child can grow to become the best version of themselves and in doing so experience a meaningful understanding of what it means to be an effective parent.

Notable Quotes About Parenting

"Children Must Be Taught How To Think, Not What To Think."

– Margaret Mead

"It's easier to build strong children than to fix broken men [or women]."

- Frederick Douglass

"Truly great friends are hard to find, difficult to leave, and impossible to forget."

– George Randolf

"Nothing in life is to be feared, it is only to be understood. Now is the time to understand more, so that we may fear less."

– Scientist Marie Curie

Table of Contents

Introduction

From changing diapers to getting kids to school on time, it feels like there is never a moment to just stop, enjoy their growth, and appreciate how fast they are learning about the world around them. Parenting is tough—everyone knows that. But you know what everyone doesn't know? It's super rewarding, too.

Every day, when you wake those tiny people in their beds, listen to their "My stomach hurts" stories about skipping school, and get them ready for the day ahead, you wonder how much longer they will need you to take care of them. People say time flies by, and right now, you wish it would. Yet when it does, all you are left with is wishful thinking. I wish I could have spent more time with them—enjoyed more, laughed more, and celebrated more.

We wish we could have made the most of the time we had with them because they flew from the cuckoo's nest. After they leave, we realize how little we see of them. Phone calls and video chats become shorter and are always interrupted by someone else's call or message. Life gets in the way. They achieve bigger things in life and only visit when they can or must. You never believed this would happen to you because you always thought you were all so close to one another. However, a friend took your precious spot over and then a romantic partner, a roommate, and finally, their soulmate. You become this unimportant part of their lives and begin wondering where you went wrong.

Well, here's what you are: You are not engaging in activities that bond you together for a lifetime. You are not creating memories to give them something to think about when they are sad and lonely. You are not scheduling alone time with them to get to know them better, listen to them, validate their feelings, and assure them that they will get their life together eventually. You are communicating but not communicating well. You are listening but only to what they are telling you—not noticing their body language, facial expressions, and gestures. You are quick to point out when they do something wrong but rarely appreciate and celebrate their small wins.

When children feel neglected emotionally by their parents, they look for those qualities and support in their peers and educators. They seek acceptance and validation from another place. They make plans to get away from you on weekends so that they can do something fun with their friends. Why can't they have fun with you? Why do you think they feel you are only their parent and not their friend?

In this book, we explore the different angles and activities that help parents connect, communicate, and form a strong bond with their child. We learn strategies as well as discuss ideas to get started. We talk about how, by spending some quality time with our children, we can impart some wisdom and life skills in them. We learn how we can be a parent and a friend at the same time and let children feel like they can always rely on you for any type of advice and suggestion.

Together, let's learn what it means to become attached. Let's learn how we can raise children that appreciate the closeness in relationships and aspire to have a similar bond with their children one day.

Chapter 1:

Healthy Bonding

A healthy bond signifies compatibility between two people. It reveals how interested and supportive they are of each other's passions, likes, and dreams. It signifies one's need for reliance and affection. A parent-child relationship (PCR) is above every other. It is a bond created between two human beings—both relying on each other for support and affection. One has a bigger part to play—from carrying the baby to birthing it. But this bond isn't just with the mother. It is equally dear and precious to the father. After all, it is equal parts him, and therefore, the responsibility to ensure its safety, care, and fulfillment of basic needs also comes to him.

However, blood binds don't mean that they will have a healthy relationship between them. Relationships require effort and commitment. They require sacrifice, respect, and availability. They require an individual who will listen to the other without judgment and bias. It involves two parties who are loyal, honest, and transparent with one another. They both deserve compassion and empathy. They both deserve to be heard and listened to. They deserve to be counted on when making important decisions. They require attachment but also independence at the same time.

When we talk about a parent-child bond and how it can be a healthy one, the first thing that parents need to work on is knowing the sort of relationship they have with their child. You might think that every parent-child relationship must be the same, but it isn't the case. Some parents have a hard time expressing their love for their children in the most apt way. For some, loving their children is about protecting them from all that is evil which is fine. However, in doing so, they often realize that they end up imposing many rules on their children which makes them hate their parents. Similarly, some are too outgoing and give their children so much liberty that the line between who's in control vanishes, and the child has no structure or routines to follow.

Research shows that early bonding has a long-term effect on a child's mental health (Winston & Chicot, 2016). How we treat them and what they receive in terms of love makes them resilient and confident in themselves. Therefore, let's assess the type of relationships there are, and which ones can resonate with you the most.

What Type of Parent-Child Relationship Do You Have?

Every parent has a different type of attachment to their child. Some encourage their children to go explore, as they take a backseat, while others look for teachable moments. Ideally, we can define a parent-child relationship in the following categories. We also know these as attachment categories.

Secure Relationship

Secure relationships are the strongest type of attachment. In this relationship, a child feels secure. They can easily depend on their parents for all their needs without hesitation. The parent also willingly addresses every need of the child—no matter how obscure and outrageous. They both know of each other's expectations. A child also feels free and confident to bond with people their age. If they are young, they may cry when they see their primary caregiver leave the room but settle down when they see a friendly face. A child is happiest when the parent picks them up from school/the nursery.

Avoidant Relationship

In avoidant relationships, there is little security involved. In this form of attachment, the child knows that there is no point depending on the parent, as they can't make them feel secure or give them what they want. Therefore, they rely on themselves for all their needs and demands. Avoidant children become independent too quickly. They get frustrated easily and don't ask for help when in need. They don't do well in social settings, especially when around other children their age. They can be aggressive and resort to biting, pushing, hitting, and screaming. These children have a difficult time building a strong and healthy bond with their parents or caregivers. They don't greet their parents when they leave or return and don't complain about the lack of attention and affection they receive. They have this sense of wanting to punish their parents, and as a result, they avoid and ignore them.

Unorganized Relationship

An unorganized relationship is one where the child isn't aware of what to expect from their parents. In the other forms of relationships, children have organized attachments. This means that they have learned ways to get what they want—even when it isn't the best way. This happens because a child learns how to predict their parent's reaction. They know how their parents will react when they do certain things.

In an unorganized relationship, children do what makes sense to them—even when they make little sense to others. They will speak really loud and fast, making it hard for the parents and caregivers to understand. They will have a meltdown or freeze in their footsteps for no obvious reason. They have a difficult time bonding with other children their age because they don't know what to make of their feelings. Unorganized children give their parents a hard time in understanding them from day one.

Ambivalent Relationship

Ambivalent relationships involve children who are insecurely attached to their parents. Children in this type of relationship have learned that their needs will sometimes be met and sometimes remain unmet. They are quick to notice what behavior gets their parents interested in the past and use it sparingly. They actively seek that sense of security they seldom receive from their parents. Ambivalent children are very clingy. They rely on their parents for most things by acting younger than they are. They can also be overly emotional and therefore require more attention. When they are angry, they may talk back and/or talk like a baby. They cry a lot, get frustrated over small things, and want to be the center of attention at all times. They get upset when made to do things on their own. They love to latch on to everyone. They have a difficult time letting go of their parents when dropped off at school at a young age.

Which of these attachment styles do you most relate to? Are you the outgoing, casual, and fun parent that lets their children do whatever they want to do, or are you the kind that ensures you meet all your child's needs?

Knowing the type of relationship and attachment there is between you two will help you learn how to make it better. The goal should be to create a secure relationship where there is a solid give and take of things. If you feel your relationship is more ambivalent, try strategies that will allow your child to act mature and take responsibility. We can achieve this when you set healthy expectations and boundaries with them to ensure they know what type of behavior we expect of them.

Why Does My Child Feel Distant?

"She doesn't share everything with me."

"I have to ask him how his school was. He never tells me about how his day went on his own."

An emotionally distant child isn't a teenager trying to find their place in the world by branching out and making new friends. It is one that purposely distances themselves from their family—friends or no friends. Parents think they have hidden things without realizing that they may be the one causing the reaction.

Maybe they are just realizing how controlling you are or how you like to make everything about yourself. How do you guilt them into doing what you want them to do? How do they feel unwanted, unappreciated, and invalidated? How do you make them keep their opinions to themselves whenever there is a big family decision at stake?

Becoming independent is a natural and healthy developmental process. It shows that a child feels confident enough to handle things on their own and manage their life better. It depicts that they are ready to trust in others the same way they trust their family members. It exhibits their need for increased social interactions which leads to picking up many positive habits.

We all want our children to grow up to be independent and self-reliant adults. However, we need to reassess our assumptions about connection. To remain connected doesn't mean staying in touch all the time. It doesn't mean spending all your time together. Staying connected means never losing touch of someone in your thoughts and prayers. It's about wanting to call them the minute something good or bad happens because you can't wait to tell them. It's about taking out the time to spend time with them, prioritizing them over work and other commitments. It's about listening and being heard.

So what are we doing wrong? How are we causing the rift? Why does it feel like our children no longer need us? Here are some ways that you may be intentionally making them pull away from you.

You Treat Them Like a Two Year Old

If your child is a tween and still treated like you would treat a toddler, they are going to get annoyed. The most favorite game of any child is to play as an adult. Even if they aren't, they want to act older and be independent. Treating them like a toddler would make them feel like they are being controlled. Their opinions remain neglected which makes them think you don't respect them. Even if they act all childish, they expect to be treated like an adult.

You Smother Them

There is a difference between being close to someone and smothering them. Parents often make mistakes between the two. Your child's definition of being smothered may differ greatly from what you have in mind. For example, they may think that you smother them with questions, criticism, and rules, whereas you think you are just being protective of them. The more smothered they feel, the larger their urge to flee.

You Are Too Critical of Them

If your child feels you pick them apart every time they are downstairs for dinner or some leisure, they are going to try to avoid you altogether. This doesn't play well in the long run when they start a job or family. If they feel that there will be nothing good enough for you, they will try to leave you and stay apart as much as possible. Therefore, hold your horses, and try to see where they are coming from. They are inexperienced with handling crises, so give them some room to be themselves. Correcting them and telling them, "I told you so" is only going to make them detest you.

You Provide an Unpleasant Environment

If you and your partner have unresolved issues to deal with, it will affect your child's mental well-being, too. Having to witness parents yelling at each other, disrespecting each other's opinions, and ridiculing their personality, the child's thoughts are fueled with negativity. An unpleasant home is an opportunity for your child to remain distant, as they don't want to be picking sides and playing the judge. An unhappy environment is one of the driving factors of why teenagers want to move out as soon as they can to get away from all that negativity.

You Don't Listen to Them

Children need to know that their thoughts, ideas, and questions matter—no matter how stupid they may sound. They need that sense of validation from you. They want to be seen as adults—even when small. They want to be told that they are smart, clever, and creative. Not taking out the time to spend with your child and listening to them is another major turnoff for your child. If you are unavailable or act like their ideas are stupid, they are going to keep them to themselves for the next time.

Becoming More Connected

Forming a strong connection with your child is the crux of a healthy bond. A high-quality parent-child relationship promotes healthy development (American Psychological Association, 2009). There has to be a strong connection or else children won't follow the rules set for them voluntarily. One of the easiest ways to strengthen a parent-child bond is by positively interacting with them in your daily routines.

For example, you must invest your time and effort. Kids may physically grow, but the entire mental and emotional growth takes place with the help of their primary caregivers. A healthy growth is possible when both parents invest their time and energy into raising a resilient, confident, and mature child. The likelihood of picking good habits and behaviors from you increases when they spend time with you. You may say that you are already spending all your free time with them, but doing their chores, feeding them, or helping them with homework isn't qualitative time. Reading with them, doing activities, and listening to them is.

You must also prioritize their needs and wants above all things. Your child shouldn't feel like they are in the backseat. They should feel loved, appreciated, and important. It isn't just your words that do the trick; your actions should align with them, too. Therefore, don't find free time in your schedule for them. Sort your schedule around them.

As a parent, you must also be available. This isn't true for their physical needs alone, like eating, cleaning, and sleeping. You must also be available to listen to and communicate. You must be attentive and prepared to see things from their point of view as well.

Talk to them, not at them, to establish trust. Conversations with your children should leave them feeling uplifted, inspired, and happy. This begins with listening to what they have to say and then offering solutions when they ask for them. Some parents feel that voicing out negative feedback constitutes back talking. However, not all feedback is negative. Allowing them to speak their minds freely makes them feel like they have a voice—an important one. It builds their confidence.

Empathize with them. Encourage expression of feelings and emotions. If your child feels shy, initiate. Talk about how your day went, what problems you tackled, how you made the most of your time, what conversations you had with your best friends, etc. When they are ready to open up, lend them a compassionate ear. Show them that their worries are your worries, and find a solution together. See things from their perspective to grasp what they are going through and how you could help them.

Be a supporter of your child—no matter what. Young ones need constant encouragement. They are just starting school and in need of a boost to ensure that everything will be alright. Encouragement and motivation from a parent boosts their self-esteem and builds confidence while criticism and correction don't.

Finally, there should be mutual respect between the two of you. Respecting your child means respecting their opinions, ideas, and people they hang out with. You must respect their needs, preferences, and dreams—even if they seem unrealistic. The idea is to make them believe you trust in their judgment and believe that they are big enough to manage their life efficiently.

There are many ways to ensure that your child feels connected. In the following chapters, we will talk about seven such activities that involve the whole family and are ideal for strengthening the bond between a parent and a child.

Chapter 2:

Eating Together

Eating together as a family encourages togetherness. There are many benefits to sharing meals with your child. According to one study, sharing meals frequently with your children is linked with better family functioning; improved social and emotional health; and stronger relationships between the parent and the child (Utter et al., 2018). Positive family mealtimes give children a sense of belonging. It makes them feel safe, loved, and valued. Mealtimes also make for an excellent opportunity to teach a young child basic table manners. They can learn about table setting, cutting into their food gracefully, and chewing their bites properly.

This promotes healthy social expectations at the table when eating with others or at a restaurant. They can learn to value the food in front of them and be thankful for it. Mealtimes are also great at promoting communication and discussing important problems. It can be a time for the parents to act as a friend and mentor/help their children deal with their school-related concerns.

Eating together as a family fosters well-adjusted, happy children. When families eat together, children feel accepted. They don't need validation or approval from the wrong crowd because they can rely on the sound judgment of their loved ones. These children seem to exhibit better social skills. Their ability to navigate social situations also improves. This is possible because of the security blanket of the family.

Adolescents also report better self-esteem and greater confidence. This was further explored in a 2015 study involving a group of Canadian researchers. Their findings reveal that frequent meal times prevent eating disorders in children, as their diet is well-balanced. They also are less likely to engage in substance abuse and violent behavior, as we address their concerns in a friendly environment. They are also less likely to become depressive and suicidal, as they feel supported and encouraged to see the positives in life (Harrison et al., 2015).

Children who eat meals with their family also do well in school. The earlier study also suggests that children who have at least six to seven meals per week with their family do better academically than children who consume fewer meals with their families. This proves that eating together isn't just a bond-strengthening affair; it also helps children excel in school.

Since mealtimes make for some healthy conversation to take place, it exposes young minds to issues that are new and unexplored by them. The dinner table can be a safe place to question and be expressive of their ideas. By being able to express themselves in front of the family and being appreciated by them, children feel more confident in expressing them with their peers and educators. They can also learn extra words and terminologies which improve their listening and reading skills. According to one study, which followed children from infancy to age 10, revealed that parents who promote eating together raise children with better health, impressive social skills, and excellent communication skills (Harbec & Pagani, 2018).

It also gives parents an insight into their child's world, which friends they have, what problems they are facing, what subjects they are finding difficult to study, or if there are any deadlines or upcoming events they need to know about.

Finally, children who eat with their families develop a positive relationship with food. They are more likely to include more fruits and vegetables in their diet and rely on fewer takeout meals and processed food (Walton et al., 2018).

It's Not Just About Eating!

The reason we believe eating together as a family is magical and effective is because there are three decades of research supporting the idea. We now know that children who eat with their families are more likely to do good in school; have resilience and confidence; are less likely to engage in illegal and harmful habits like drugs and alcohol; and develop better eating habits and table manners.

Yet eating together doesn't just involve gathering around the table and consuming a meal. It can be a learning saga for children to take up positive life skills.

For example, where does the food that we eat come from? Who prepares the meal, cooks it, and then sets it? Who is responsible for deciding what produce is best for the family, especially for the kids? Who sets the menu, who gets the groceries, or who makes the list?

In short, eating isn't just a one-time affair. It is an excellent way to teach children about table etiquettes, money management, goal setting, and improving conversation skills. If you don't believe me, then look for yourself.

When you first decide to prepare a meal, what is the one thing you need? Produce. From different spices to vegetables and meat, a meal needs all these and more to become one. So you take out a pen and write down all the things you need from the store. You get your child engaged, and they can help you prepare the list. You can even expand on the various food groups by sectioning out similar items; for example, under meat, you have crab, salmon, chicken thighs, and wings etc.; under vegetables, you have green peppers, cabbage, lettuce, and frozen peas; and under spices, you have cumin, turmeric, garlic powder, etc.

This is a suitable example of setting a goal by clearly defining all the objectives. Your children can learn to apply the same technique to prepare for their exams and chores. They can divide a single task into many smaller tasks and take on them one by one.

What comes next after you have a list? Going to the store. Once there, you can help your child pick from the many brands there are on the shelves and go through the labels. This requires critical thinking because they have to decide based on the many narratives they have. As soon as you have everything in the cart, next comes going to the cashier and having everything checked out. You can encourage your child to handle the expenses and know how much everything costs. This will instill a good habit of money management and seeing how everything comes at a price.

Once you are home, you organize and put things in their designated places which teaches children better organization skills and why they should keep everything clean. You can throw in a few tips about how to keep the bread fresh, how to prevent the milk from going bad, how to stock up vegetables so they remain fresh for longer, etc.

When it comes to preparing a meal, it takes more than one person to help. You can have your child help you with cutting the vegetables, making a salad, squeezing some lemon juice, etc. When they feel involved, it will nurture excellent cooking skills in them which is a great life skill. When they see you clean up after everyone has finished eating, they learn the value of keeping the kitchen clean and how to do it.

In between, they eat the meal they have helped cook, set the table, and spend some quality time with their parents and talk about their day or anything significant.

Overall, family meals aren't just a one-time thing: They are much more than that!

Making Mealtimes Enjoyable

With life getting in the way, it can be difficult for parents to sit together with their children and have dinner as a family. However, given the benefits, you must try to make it work. For starters, if the idea of preparing a meal from scratch worries you, delegate a task to everyone to help you. Your partner can take over with cutting vegetables, and your children can wash them and set the table while you cook. You can also share the responsibility of doing the dishes among yourselves to avoid cleaning up alone.

Also, you can schedule mealtimes. You can set up a weekly schedule to ensure everyone is there. You can also set rules around the table such as no phone usage, finishing everything on the plate, chewing without noise, etc. Also, be sure to plan your activities before mealtime so that there is no rush to finish up. You must give children at least 20 minutes to enjoy their meal completely. Having more relaxation time encourages trying new foods and building good eating habits. Having more time on their hands also means that children can be mindful of what they are eating; how the different textures and spices enrich their palate; and then appreciate the meal. If you have young children, they will have a difficult time sitting for that long. Allow them to move around a little, but stress on eating their food while sitting, as it reduces the chances of them choking on their food as they run around.

To make mealtimes more enjoyable and exciting, you can design food menus and take out your best crockery. You can ask children to pretend to be servers and serve you food like waiters do in restaurants.

For younger children who are picky eaters, you can mask healthy nutrients in their favorite foods, like adding some carrots in their mashed potatoes or blending kale and strawberries in a smoothie together. You can also cut foods into unique and creative shapes, taking some inspiration from websites like Pinterest.

You can also make mealtimes more fun by developing a theme around it. For example, some nights can be pasta nights where you cook pasta with different sauces. Some mealtimes can be taco nights where you try different taco fillings and seasonings. You can also make burgers from scratch and call it a burger fest. You can also get more creative by ditching the good old table and setting up a picnic in the backyard. You can put up some lights and play some tunes in the background to enjoy your meal.

With young children, let them get messy. Some toddlers throw a fit because they want to eat like an adult.

Encourage that—they only want to learn more. Give them those cute, child-friendly utensils and their own plate. Cut their food into small pieces and let them eat. They will drop some on the floor, and get some on their clothes, but they will actually enjoy the meal. If you try to take charge or yell, they will associate eating with negative feelings and give you an even harder time in the future.

Chapter 3:

Taking up a DIY Project

Children have become more tech-savvy than ever before. They spend most of their free time browsing social media or taking selfies. According to various statistics, teenagers spend roughly five to seven hours using their phones every day. This means that the time previously spent on interacting with physical objects, drafting, or creating something that enhances their coordination skills goes wasted. Due to lack of interest and the ease of getting everything ready, schools have omitted courses on home improvement and home economics. However, relying solely on schools to teach life skills to children is absurd, too. They need to learn basic survival skills like how to cook, clean, and take care of themselves.

Luckily, there is a great way to encourage children to learn these without ever needing to attend a class for it.: a do-it-yourself (DIY) project. It can be a home improvement project, like building a shelf together, assembling furniture, or setting up a birdhouse for birds during dry summers. Projects require healthy discussions so that everyone is aware of the plan; they also require coordination and teamwork so that tasks are completed efficiently. Not to mention, they make for some amazing bonding time for the child and the parent, leading to many happy memories and sometimes even disasters. In this chapter, we discuss how taking up a project can make room for some one-on-one time with your child and how you can impart wisdom and teach some life lessons.

A DIY project allows children to express themselves through their creativity and imagination. The project can be as simple as watering the plants or creating a water dispenser for your dog using plastic bottles and some cardboard. Having a means to express themselves artistically is beneficial for young children. For instance, it helps them find their passions and interests. They can spend some quality time learning a new art and hone their skills at it. They can improve their hand-eye coordination by focusing on the many steps of creating something from scratch.

If you feel you may not have the time to take on a full-on project like building a treehouse with your child, a simple project confined to one small area in your house can be a great start. The easier the project, the sooner it will be finished. The sooner they complete it, the happier they will be. They will be overjoyed with a sense of accomplishment for having achieved something they set their mind to. Longer projects may make kids lose interest and become discouraged when they don't see end results.

Why DIY?

According to Tara Dennis (2020), a renowned interior decorator who has worked with big firms like 3M, Samsung, and Plush Sofas, etc., nurturing a child's creative side is as important as allowing them to play outdoor games and reading. A DIY creative project helps develop sensory stimulation, hone their motor skills, and promote imagination and creative thinking. Upon completing a DIY project successfully, they are left with the sense of pride that they, too, can create something special.

Craft-related activities are excellent for children. They require a dedicated amount of patience and concentration which promotes problem-solving and free thinking. When partnered with a companion like a parent or sibling, it can be incredibly fun and relaxing. Together, they can brainstorm new ideas and create something close to them.

DIY projects are labor-free projects. You start them on your own, at your own expense, after calculating a desired budget. You do everything from purchasing the materials to setting up and working on it while remaining engaged. There are many times when you think something would look better if you gave it a personal touch, and it does. Now, imagine your child is on board with you by looking and admiring the entire process and how you pay attention to it.

Apart from their cognitive development, DIYs encourage children to figure out things for themselves. If they feel stuck at any point, they can go back and brainstorm another way again, fostering problem-solving. With more children in the house, together you can all put your heads together and come up with a plan that everyone agrees with and create something innovative.

When children partner with their parents, we can assign them simple tasks like lifting and moving things. This will improve their hand-eye coordination, dexterity, and motor skills. They will learn how to control their hands and fingers. They will learn the best ways to lift something and use their shoulders, elbows, and waist for support.

Another great thing about DIYs is that there is no age limit. There are thousands of DIY projects that you can undertake with your young one after noticing their interest and age. For example, if they seem interested in knitting and tie-dyeing, you can start with basic stitches and big wools to make learning easier. You can also use nontoxic paints and ask them to paint a shirt. From there, you can move on to a more complex process once they learn the basics and are ready to try something new and interesting.

Finally, a DIY project gives children something else other than screen time to think about. It gets them moving and doing things as opposed to sitting on the couch watching videos all day. They can remain distracted and focused on something more valuable.

DIY projects are also great for hyperactive children who have a moderately poor attention span. They can remain absorbed and utilize most of their energy in doing something meaningful.

Getting Started: What Projects to Pick

Since everything is readily available in shops today, it's hard to come up with a project that is age appropriate for your child, related to something they are interested in, and fulfills an inner need. Children at different developmental stages have different needs. In this final section, we focus on how to pick the best projects for your child, considering all these factors mentioned above.

Age-Appropriate Projects for Children Aged 0 to 3

Children in this age group strongly need to become empowered. They may be too young to build a shelf or use any of the wielding tools, but they will try to get their hands on everything. This suggests a need for empowerment and independence. Ideal projects for them will be:

- Watering plants using a kid-sized watering can
- Setting the dinner table
- Digging holes to plant seedlings

- Sweeping and mopping the floor using a kid-sized broom and mop
- Helping to hammer a nail by using a toy hammer

Age-Appropriate Projects for Children Aged 3 to 5

At this stage, children demand more independence and ownership. They want to do things their way and create a space and name for themselves. Ideal projects to keep them engaged in include:

- Creating artwork
- Assisting with paint stirring when painting furniture or walls
- Holding the tape measure when checking the length and width of items
- Folding table napkins and laundry
- Making binoculars from empty toilet paper rolls

Age-Appropriate Projects for Children Aged 5 to 8

As children start elementary school, their need for independence further increases. They seek their identity and what represents them. Projects that resonate with their interests and who they are make for excellent DIYs and quality bonding time. Here are some ideas:

- A DIY organizer using egg cartons for trinkets and other jewelry
- Building a hanging shelf for their toys and books
- Painting a pot for the garden and planting a seed in it
- Making a bigger organizer using a shoebox or cardboard box
- Baking a simple cupcake by mixing all ingredients

Age-Appropriate Projects for Children Aged 8 to 12

Kids this age need ownership. They are more likely to move into a bigger bedroom that they can call their own. An excellent way to spend some quality time with them would be to help them assemble their new furniture, hang murals, and set the room up. Some ideas for a DIY include:

- Creating a list of the items needed for the room
- Painting a wall
- Hammering nails into an artwork for the wall
- Creating a no-sew pillow for their bed
- Helping with raking fallen leaves

Age-Appropriate Projects for Children Aged 12 to 15

Around this age, the goal should be to instill some responsibility in them. You can do this by assigning them chores in the house and taking care of the laundry, etc. Some other ideas include:

- Building a birdhouse using a kit
- Repainting old furniture
- Setting up a pathway using round stones
- Following instructions on how to set up IKEA furniture
- Fixing a leaky faucet or squeaky door

Chapter 4:

Volunteer Work

Parents today face an arduous battle because children don't show interest in anything besides burying their faces into the screens of a phone. They only put them down when told. Their engagement with the world around them has become restricted. If we go back three or four decades ago and recall our childhood, our finest memories include the time we spent playing outdoors, helping our friends fix a busted bicycle tire, playing hopscotch, jumping rope, and going to the arcade to play some games. Children today don't even bother knowing the children their age in their neighborhood. They will gladly befriend them on social media channels like Facebook and Snapchat but rarely take the time out to engage in physical one-on-one interaction.

Losing human touch also means that their contribution toward their community is zero. By restricting themselves to the online world, they miss out on the joy that comes from giving and helping others. Community welfare is everyone's job. Volunteerism sets an excellent example of how children can contribute to society positively and in return, learn about kindness, empathy, and compassion.

Helping others feels good. The pride and satisfaction of having made someone's life a little easier is the primary reason people volunteer. The act of volunteering requires commitment and engagement. You learn to respect and value what you have. You come face-to-face with the problems that others meet in their daily lives and realize how blessed you truly are.

There are many benefits to volunteerism. For starters, it strengthens the community. Nonprofit organizations may do their part, but we also must ensure that everyone within our community leads a peaceful and happy life.

It also strengthens your family as a unit. Working together to bring happiness to the face of others is a great way to spend a fun weekend. It can help children see the efforts and pains parents go through to provide for their family. They can appreciate their role and offerings and be grateful.

The Act of Giving

Engaging children in volunteering activities from an early age can encourage sharing and helping others. It teaches them a sense of responsibility toward others. Volunteering requires commitment as stated earlier. Becoming associated with a charitable organization or donation drive can teach young kids about accountability. They can also learn time management skills as they have to make time from their schedules to give to others. They feel responsible for providing for others in their community with no prejudice or bias.

Young children also learn how their efforts can bring happiness to others. Many times, we hesitate in extending our hands to others because we believe that one individual alone can't make a difference. However, volunteering can change their mind. It becomes visible to them how their contribution, no matter how trivial, brings a smile to someone's face. Giving as little as $10 to someone on the streets can help them buy some necessities.

Volunteering also teaches young children about tolerance. They get to meet people from all walks of life, as well as sexual orientation, race, or religion. When this happens, children must remain objective and help everyone wholeheartedly. They must put aside their views and help everyone equally. This act also teaches children to be more appreciative and accepting of the people who look different from them. It shows them that, given a common cause, we can all unite and stay harmoniously.

Volunteering for charitable causes can also help children prosper in their academics. They can decide on what future career they want to pursue. For instance, some children might show more interest in volunteering at a pet shelter. Their desire to help animals might encourage them to become a vet. Similarly, if a child shows more interest in the organization and marketing of a charitable institution, like driving a social campaign around the neighborhood and school, they can opt for a career in business and management. If they seem more driven toward helping others get better, they may join the medical field.

When children team up with other children and parents, they learn about the value of teamwork and cooperation. They can come up with some excellent ideas to raise donations for the needy and take up many leadership roles as well.

Finally, they can make the best use of their idle time and energy. They can pack food parcels, clothes, and old books to give away and use their time more wisely.

Making Volunteering a Family Pursuit

Children follow in their parent's footsteps most of the time. They pick up their behaviors and habits. It won't be wrong to say that they fill in your shoes. It is a chance to instill good habits in them—the type of habits that will make you proud of them. Therefore, if you want them to pursue volunteerism in their lives, now is the time to set a good example. You must be at the forefront. Children should see you helping others passionately. You can't preach to the choir and remain indifferent. Your actions should be louder than your words. Discuss instances with them where you helped someone. Emphasize the experience and what satisfaction it brought you. Talk about how the act of giving had a valuable return.

Once they seem interested and willing to take part, research opportunities where you can volunteer as a family. Several organizations host events to raise donations, like marathons and auctions. Get involved in them and take your child along. Expose them to the act firsthand and notice how they respond.

You can always start small and set weekly goals. On some weekends, you can help pick up garbage from a park near you. You can even run a beach cleanup drive, and ask your friends and family to join you. You can make a whole day out of it and spend some quality time together. Such contributions don't require spending a lot of money. You can just purchase some garbage bags and gloves and get started. Later, you can drop the garbage at a recycling plant and see the collected trash be recycled.

Another great idea can be to help repair and renovate houses of low-income residents near you. You can help them stock up on some basics like clothing, food, and furniture. You can paint their homes and repair some broken furniture.

You and your child can also volunteer in a soup kitchen and serve the homeless a nice meal. You can find an organization that does that and go to offer additional help.

You can also take your child to a senior citizen's nursing home and have them spend the day there. You can even organize a small event like a talent show. You can also volunteer to plant trees and flowers at your nearest park and get other children from the neighborhood also involved.

You and your child can pack care packages for homeless shelter residents that contain toiletries and clean clothes. Once all the packages are ready, you can drive around and have your child give them away to the homeless people you meet and witness the joy on their faces.

During fall, you can volunteer to clean the yards of your neighbors that are old, have had surgery, or have recently become a parent. You can rake leaves, pick up sticks, and catch debris from their lawns and driveways to ensure safety. If they have welcomed a new baby, you can volunteer to help them with the house chores or look after the baby with your child. They can also give away the toys and clothes they have outgrown.

Chapter 5:

Plan a Picnic or a Hike

Vacations and picnics are fun for the whole family. When life fills up with responsibilities, it is okay to get away and enjoy a little. From running errands to running on the beach; folding laundry to drying clothes in the air; or cooking to eating prepacked foods, picnics make for a great escape for the whole family. When on a vacation, no matter how small, parents can bond with their children in a new light—minus the worry. Life can slow down and take a breather, promising you some quality time to spend together with your little one.

Picnics and family outings make everyone happy. No one has ever returned from a vacation feeling unhappy. Having some break from work and school activities can help both parents and children enjoy themselves. Vacations and picnics help individuals return with more excitement and productivity levels. They feel more energized. They experience clarity of things and also report healthier relationships.

People tend to return from vacation happier and more relaxed. No surprise there, but many various studies show that these same people were more productive and had closer family relationships.

A planned getaway has considerable benefits for a child's development. Family getaways provide children with mental health advantages. They gain firsthand knowledge of what it takes to plan, organize, and execute a successful trip. The more experienced they become at planning, the more confident they become about their management skills. It builds their focus and gives their creativity a nudge.

The word picnic practically implies a time to relax and unwind. Stress reduction is the fruitful result one can enjoy. Children can unplug from their problems with peers and teachers and relieve some stress. This type of reset button reduces stress which results in better immunity and overall well-being.

Picnics can also be fun and knowledgeable. When a child goes on any type of excursion or school trip, they learn about the place they are visiting, why it's significant, what type of crowd comes there, what to take back from that place, etc. For example, when schools plan trips, they usually take children to a historic or informative spot, like a national monument, planetarium, or museum. Going there and witnessing its grandeur allows children to learn about that place and what makes it special. Also, they get to go with their friends and create some amazing memories.

Besides, it isn't just the trip that is a cause for excitement; it is the entire process of planning and executing it.

The Art of Planning, Organizing, and Execution

The art of planning a picnic or trip is serious business. It can be as exciting as you want it to be or as boring as you want it. To successfully plan and execute a family trip, there are some steps that you must follow.

Start by picking an ideal location for a family-oriented trip. After deciding how many days you want to spend on a vacation, plan the destination accordingly. Get your children involved in the decision-making process and encourage them to take an active part in the planning. For starters, they can help you pick a place based on their interests. If they are more into history, a trip to a destination that boasts historical architecture will be an amazing idea. If they are the fun and outdoorsy type, a day at a theme park or carnival will be best. If they love nature, going to a place where they can marvel at its beauty in the best manner should be on the list. In this respect, you can go on a small hike together, plan a camping trip, or go to the beach for a day of fun.

Once you have the location and number of days jotted down, the next step involves creating a packing list. What are you going to take along? Again, it depends on where you are going and what type of weather you can expect. Children, especially of a young age, love to be a part of the packing process, as it shows them that things are moving fast. Ask them to create an individual list for their clothes, shoes, and other accessories they would like to pack. If possible, you can also help them set a bag or suitcase that carries only their things. Being responsible for their own luggage instills a sense of responsibility in them.

Once you pack suitcases, you must decide on a menu and ask your children to help around with the preparation. You can take them to the grocery store to buy the stuff you need, and then, you can ask for their help in the kitchen doing small stuff. There are tons of simple picnic recipes you can browse and take along for the ride.

Once that is out of the way, create another list to ensure that you have packed all the essentials, like medication, toiletries, documents, etc. If you are going for an extended vacation to another country, get any vaccinations you might need upon arrival.

Appreciate your child for all their hard work, commitment, and assistance with the packing and planning once you are on your way. Emphasize how their presence and involvement made things so much easier for you. This will boost their confidence and self-worth.

Once you reach the destination, enjoy as much as you can as a family. Relax and communicate. Talk about the things you never get to talk about at home, as you take in the beautiful views of the destination.

Go Out... But Where?

There are different places and trips you can take with your children. You don't always have to plan a trip across or outside the country. The idea is to plan a simple getaway where you can have some quality, worry-free time from working with your young ones and know what's going on in their lives. The trip should involve something that helps you two connect and feel joyous about. Below are some ideas for the type of trip you can take with your family and what you can expect from them:

Camping: A trip in the wild offers children a heightened sense of appreciation for nature and all the beauty that surrounds them. You can talk about its conservation and protection by ensuring to keep the waters and land clean. Camping also teaches kids self-sufficiency. In the world, you can never know what's going to happen next. It also makes you appreciate all the luxuries we take for granted in our homes such as air conditioning, TV, and the Internet. On the trip, children can pick up some great survival skills such as how to hunt, start a fire, and look after any injuries they acquire.

Beach: A trip to the beach allows children to breathe in the fresh air, roll in the sand, make sandcastles, collect seashells, and learn about the many fishes that rule the waters. They can learn to appreciate the views of the pristine waters in front of them and take in all that beautiful sight. Once there, it may be a good time to encourage them to keep the beach clean and pick up any garbage they find.

Park: A visit to the park makes for a great bonding activity for children their age. It is a great idea to practice their social skills and interact with other children. Chances are, they will come across children from different communities, ethnicities, and races. Playing with them will foster acceptance and appreciation for them. It also fosters learning about different cultures and people. Together, children can come up with new games and be creative.

Museums: Going to a museum may not feel like a fun trip, but it can be highly beneficial for young kids. Museums facilitate learning. Children gain a deeper, conceptual understanding of their history, cultures, and people. They take in the information using all their senses, like touch, sight, smell, hearing, and taste. Museums are a hub of information. They nurture curiosity, and they enlighten young people about evolution and the struggles one had to face in the old days. Museums can make room for some interesting conversation and topics that spark imagination and help children learn about unknown worlds.

Chapter 6:

Schedule Game Nights on Weekends

Not long ago, there was a time when families used to spend their weekends playing board games and fun activities. They would sit around the table, face each other, and play real-life, interactive games. The winner would rejoice and scream with excitement while losers would have to show sportsmanship and not lose heart. Then, another game would start, and the same excitement would continue for hours well into the night.

Today, parents and children sit together but with phones and tablets in their hands. There is little to no engagement; no fun and laughter; and no memories to cherish later. If you recall correctly, all that lighthearted play led to some important skills development. From games like Monopoly, children learned about the importance of money and why they should spend it wisely. Games like UNO improved their strategy-building skills. Ludo taught them how to win with teamwork. Playing charades improved their hand-eye coordination and creativity. Word-building games like

Scrabble and crosswords encouraged the learning of new words and their usage.

Thinking of family involvement activities, it is time to bring game nights back and allow your children to experience the same joy we once did.

A game night equals family time. Family time is essential to build a strong sense of love. The more time parents spend with their children doing something positive, the stronger their bond will become. You don't have to go big and schedule games prior. You can just start a new tradition by suggesting playing a game by putting the phones down. As soon as they begin to have fun, they will demand another game night soon. Ultimately, this will become a family tradition for the weekends, and your kids will make sure to take time to be there. Strategize and pick games you know your child will love playing. Lose purposely when you see them losing heart and becoming distracted. The goal is to start a regimen for the weekends. You can always win the next round.

How Games Strengthen Bonds

There are many perks to scheduling game nights. They are one of the best ways to spend time with your children. Every game requires participants to interact with one another, strategize their moves, and help the other finish successfully. This interaction improves conversation and makes team players practice collaboration. By playing together, they realize they can only win if the other wins which ensures they work together as part of a team.

This can be an excellent way to connect with your children without discrimination. We have this culture where parents are close to one child. There is this sort of hesitance when speaking to a child of the opposite gender. For example, for a daughter, her father may not be the most ideal candidate to discuss period talk with. She would be more comfortable discussing it with her mother. Then, there are some topics that sons feel more comfortable speaking about with their fathers. During game nights, this distinction is eliminated, and everyone plays as an equal.

Second, parents connect well among themselves, too. Every marriage has its ups and downs. Sometimes, partners wish they could have more time to spend with one another, but going on a date night or taking a quick trip isn't always workable. In homes where children are young, it is easy to become disconnected because there is little free time. Luckily, game nights give parents some time to cool off as well and become more connected.

Sometimes, it feels like our children are becoming distant. As they grow up, they start to hide things from us. They ask us to leave the room because they are on the phone with a friend and need some privacy. Some days, they seem happy and joyous while on others, they wouldn't eat or come out of their rooms. As parents, we just want to be there for them—whether they are happy or sad. We want to be a part of their lives and break any barriers that have emerged. Family game nights are a fantastic way to do that.

With games like two truths and a lie, you can talk about stuff they won't discuss with you and have them open up. You can also assure them of your support and consideration. By teaming up with them, you can show them you will forever love them and support them in all their decisions without judgment. Opening gateways of communication in a fun manner also makes it easier for them to trust you. By helping them win and enjoy the game, they can see that you remain true to your words.

Board games, especially ones that require strategizing, can impart some valuable skills to young kids. They can learn the art of management and responsibility. When you hold them accountable for their actions and moves in a game, they realize that their decisions and actions have consequences they must now bear. This builds resilience in them and instills a sense of accountability. If they lose money in Monopoly, they can become more appreciative of their pocket money and choose to use it wisely. When they lose a game, they can learn about staying strong. It teaches them to accept their failures and mistakes with grace and elegance.

Many games also present children with real-life scenarios. Games where they have to role-play someone or escape a situation they are in teaches them how to be creative and imaginative. Such games also teach them how to survive within less and still succeed. For example, playing games with a "what-if" scenario forces them to make choices that will impact their lives. Presuming they choose to drop out of college in a game, they must be prepared to lead an average, low-income life, as people who finish college are more likely to end up with a high-income job. This way, while being in a controlled environment, children can prepare themselves for future experiences and learn how to cope with them.

Playing games that involve trivia questions and fun facts will increase their knowledge about the world and help them excel in school. When they know the answers to those questions, they will feel more confident about their intelligence.

Winning enhances happiness and uplifts one's mood. It is an ideal way to distract them from everyday struggles and stresses. They can be themselves, even for a few hours, and enjoy it to their heart's content.

Game nights also mean that phones will be put down for good, and the whole family will get to spend some quality time together. Throw in some snacks, and it will turn into a night to remember.

Game Night Ideas for the Whole Family

What games should you introduce your children to? In this last section, we briefly discuss some family-oriented, fun, and exciting games to get started. These games teach them how to play like a team, strategize, problem-solve, use analytical thinking, and use their imagination to decipher clues and riddles. These also require minimum setup and are ideal for children of all ages.

Minute to Win It: This is a widely popularized game show on TV and has a big following. As the name suggests, the player has a minute to finish a task. You can buy a kit of the game or DIY your own games using household items. For example, one game could be to pop balloons, and whichever player pops the most balloons in a minute wins. You can rack up the complexity of the challenges and track everyone's performances. You can also team up as players and play against the other team.

Pictionary: Pictionary is another fun and interesting game to play on game nights. All you need are some markers and sheets to draw on. This is mostly played among teams of two where one individual guesses what the other individual is drawing on the board. It requires quick thinking, good drawing, and fun imagination skills.

Monopoly: Even today, this game is one of the most played games. This board game involves strategizing and planning your moves. You can earn or lose money, be thrown into jail, own a house, and make important deals.

Scavenger Hunt: Scavenger hunts are an old classic and a favorite of everyone. Each team gets a list of clues they need to decipher and find items using them. Whichever team collects all the pieces first wins.

Charades: This is a guessing game where one player has to guess the name of a movie, actor, famous person, or thing by acting it out. You can make it as educational as you like by exploring famous monuments, cities, and countries. This improves a child's expression skills, as they have to make the other player guess what they are trying to say without actually saying it.

Would You Rather?: This is also a fun game that involves flashcards. You can come up with your own set of choices you want to give to the other person. Each player is presented with two scenarios. They have to choose one and then answer why they chose that. By customizing your questions, you can make it about your family, like:

- "Would you rather go on a trip with Mommy or Daddy?"
- "Would you rather go to your aunt's house or grandma's house for the holidays?"

- "Would you rather play video games all day or watch television?"

Chapter 7:

Read Together

The gift of reading is one of the best gifts you can give to your child. Instilling good reading habits early on gives them a competitive edge over children who don't read. Reading allows us to understand the struggles of everyday people. We feel understood when we read about a character going through the same hardships as we are. We feel valued and appreciated. Every new book opens a doorway to new worlds, people, and cultures. Take up a historical book, and you will learn how people lived back in the day. Pick up a science fiction book, and you can have a general idea of what the world is going to look like in the coming years. You can be in two different places at the same time as you read. The more books you read, the more you realize how others have felt scared, embarrassed, and sad, too. When you finish a book with a happy ending, you feel hopeful about your own life and circumstances.

Reading teaches us empathy, respect, comprehension, and compassion. Now, imagine how lucky we could be if we were to impart the same joy and pleasure that reading promises to our children. How blessed would they be?

Creating a daily family reading habit increases everyone's knowledge. Reading a book together can lead to some healthy discussions about right and wrong and responsibility. By discussing the story lines, the motives, and the actions of the characters, you can gain valuable insights into emotional regulation.

Reading Can Be Fun, Too

For students with exceptional vocabularies, exposure to good books early on is imperative. Repetitive exposure is what makes children memorize words and use them in a variety of contexts. Reading aloud as a family can help young children build their vocabulary as well as pronunciation. If they stumble upon a word, you can correct them and explain the meaning of that unfamiliar word. Once they can comprehend its meaning, they are likely to remember it. When children realize how quickly they are learning new words, they will learn to love reading and be more interested in the activity.

Reading together, as stated before, gives parents a chance to have conversations on difficult topics such as dating, relationships, safe sex, addiction, etc. These topics are tricky for parents to navigate, as children don't feel comfortable speaking about them openly. Reading about a character that is going through something similar can pave the way for some healthy and important conversation about it. When families feel comfortable speaking about them, children can be more expressive around them.

Reading as a family also exposes children to new adventures and experiences. Life happens, and everyone interprets things differently. By reading about common challenges such as the habit of lying, hitting others, or being disrespectful toward their cultures and identity, children can ask more questions about them and become more intellectual.

Children can also become more aware of their feelings and emotions. Nearly every children's book has a moral or lesson to it. By exploring those ideas and valuable lessons, children can feel more prepared to handle emotions, especially negative ones.

With busy school and work schedules, parents rarely get time to spend with their children. Reading, as an activity, doesn't require much time. Reading for as little as 15 minutes can strengthen the bond between a parent and a child. Together, they can share a laugh by enacting a scene from the book or by speaking in funny voices. The more enjoyable and sillier a book is, the greater the chances of it cracking them up. Laughter equals a positive experience, and soon, children will look forward to another one.

Finally, it changes their perspectives about things. When children read about people different from them, they become exposed to new cultures and traditions. They learn of their significance and why people celebrate them. This allows them to appreciate different cultures and people within their social circles and don't discriminate against them.

Finding the Best Read-Aloud Books

What books are best to read as a family? Finding books you can read aloud with your children may seem like a daunting task, especially when you have children of different ages and interests in the house. However, it isn't impossible. Many books promise wholesome and entertaining content for the whole family to enjoy over a read after dinner.

So, the next time you go book picking with your children, here are some things you must be mindful of. An ideal book should do the following:

Resonate With Your Family Dynamics: Do you have children of different ages? Are they all boys or girls? Do they have large age gaps? Do they share the same interests? Seeking answers to these questions will help you decide the type of book you want to buy. If there is a certain topic that you wish to discuss with your children, you may also consider it as a reason to purchase a book. For instance, if you want to talk about sharing and collaborative play with your toddler, you can pick books that preach about it in a fun and engaging manner.

Be Read Repeatedly: Another important characteristic you must look for in an ideal book for the family is whether you can read it over and over again or not. It should be a classic. Good books stand the test of time and can be enjoyed by people of all ages. A classic literature piece should feature a relatable character, engaging story line, dynamic writing, and universal themes. Think books along the line of *Little Women*, or *Charlotte's Web*. They are as popular today as they were when we read them.

Stimulate Their Mind and Imagination: A good book for a family should be educational. It should cover diverse topics that leave the readers with questions and curiosity in their minds. A good book should make your child wonder. It should leave them wanting to know more.

Appeal to Their Maturity and Intellectual Level: Apart from interest, you must select books that are befitting for your child's maturity and intellectual level. Pick books that apply to the experiences they are having. If your children are too young, books with illustrations and pictures will keep them interested. If they are older, books that deal with complex but important issues can be a great start.

Support Diversity: You must choose books that address issues of race, ethnicity, and the religions of characters. Being exposed to people from all walks of life makes them open-minded and accepting of them. They can experience what it is like to be in someone else's shoes and become empathetic.

Some excellent examples for such books include:

- *Rump*
- *The Giving Tree*
- *Charlotte's Web*
- *Charlie and the Chocolate Factory*
- *The Adventures of Captain Underpants*
- *Nim's Island*
- *The Velveteen Rabbit*
- *Three Times Lucky*
- *Missy Piggle-Wiggle and the Whatever Cure*
- *The Lion, the Witch, and the Wardrobe*

Conclusion

Spending quality time with your family makes for some amazing memories. In an age where technology has disconnected us from one another, we need to go back to our roots and rely on one-on-one time.

For instance, by eating together, scheduling game nights, volunteering as a family, and going on picnics, we can remind children that human interaction is above everything else.

By doing projects together, they can create something fun and unique. They can work as a team and successfully finish a DIY project that they can feel proud of. It boosts their creativity and imagination. They learn how to make the most of their time and utilize the resources they have.

By helping out the needy and running cleaning drives in the neighborhood, they can improve their social skills as well as be thankful for what they have.

By going on trips, children learn to plan and execute that plan successfully. Once there, they can learn many important life skills such as environmental conservation, surviving in the wild, and making the best of the available resources.

By reading together as a family, parents can discuss roles, story lines, and work out the struggles a protagonist faces. They can feel more prepared and knowledgeable in case they are ever in the same circumstance. Families can also talk about issues that children face at school such as bullying, discrimination, and disrespect. They can be more open about their problems with their parents and come up with solutions to solve them.

We can show them that we love them wholeheartedly and talk about things they feel uncomfortable talking about. Engaging in the seven activities we talked about in the book gives parents a chance to strengthen the bond and communicate their hopes, wishes, and expectations. In return, children can find ways to live up to their expectations by being present and engaged in these activities. They can pick some valuable lessons along the way, too. They learn about the importance of communication, listening, and transparency. By spending time with one another, they can learn to view and appreciate another person's perspective and choices.

Thank you for giving this book a read. I hope you loved reading it as much as I enjoyed writing it. It would make me the happiest person on earth if you would take a moment to leave an honest review. All you have to do is visit the site where you purchased this book: It's that simple! The review doesn't have to be a full-fledged paragraph; a few words will do. Your few words will help others decide if this is what they should be reading as well. Thank you in advance, and best of luck with your parenting adventures. Every moment is a joyous one with a child.

References

5 benefits of family game night. (2018, September 11). Froggy's Play Palace. https://www.froggysplaypalace.com/post/10-benefits-of-family-game-night

5 research-based reasons why family game nights are important. (n.d.). Info.scholarschoice.ca. https://info.scholarschoice.ca/blog/home/5-research-based-reasons-why-family-game-nights-are-important

7 reasons why D.I.Y (do it yourself) is best for your child's development & creativity. (2020, November 23). Be Cre8v. https://becre8v.com/7-reasons-why-d-i-y-do-it-yourself-is-best-for-your-childs-development-creativity/

19 family game night ideas: Have a fun night together! (2018, May 23). IFamilyKC.

https://www.ifamilykc.com/blog/things-to-do/family-game-night-ideas/

American Psychological Association. (2009, April 1). Parents and caregivers are essential to children's healthy development. *Https://Www.apa.org.* https://www.apa.org/pi/families/resources/parents-caregivers

Barnett, G. (n.d.). *9 reasons family game nights are important to parents and children.* Game Night Bros. Retrieved November 22, 2021, from https://gamenightbros.com/family-game-nights/

Brown, L. L. (2013, July 11). *Tips for volunteering with kids | parenting tips & advice.* PBS KIDS for Parents. https://www.pbs.org/parents/thrive/tips-for-volunteering-with-kids

Canning, C. (2016, August 8). *The importance of family reading.* Our Children. https://ptaourchildren.org/the-importance-of-family-reading/

Carrero, K. (2018, March 20). *Here are the 7 reasons every family should start a game night right now*. Extremely Good Parenting. https://karacarrero.com/why-start-family-game-night/

Check out these fun family game night ideas. (2020, June 25). Now from Nationwide. https://blog.nationwide.com/family-game-night-ideas/

Community service: A family's guide to getting involved (for parents) - nemours kidshealth. (n.d.). Kidshealth.org. https://kidshealth.org/en/parents/volunteer.html

Dennis, T. (2020, April 21). *Get crafty with the kids: The importance of DIY*. The Carousel. https://thecarousel.com/lifestyle/parenting/get-crafty-with-the-kids-the-importance-of-diy/

Earley, B. (2021, November 9). *The ultimate guide to "do-it-togethers" for you and your kid, no matter their age.* Apartment Therapy. https://www.apartmenttherapy.com/do-it-together-family-diy-activity-ideas-36995293

Hanz, F. (2016, November 3). *8 ways to make family meal times more fun*. Dumb Little Man. https://www.dumblittleman.com/fun-family-meals/

Harbec, M.-J., & Pagani, L. S. (2018). Associations between early family meal environment quality and later well-being in school-age children. *Journal of Developmental & Behavioral Pediatrics*, *39*(2), 136–143. https://doi.org/10.1097/dbp.0000000000000520

Harrison, M. E., Norris, M. L., Obeid, N., Fu, M., Weinstangel, H., & Sampson, M. (2015). Systematic review of the effects of family meal frequency on psychosocial outcomes in youth. *Canadian Family Physician*, *61*(2), e96–e106. https://www.ncbi.nlm.nih.gov/pmc/articles/PMC4325878/

HealthyFamilies BC. (2014, November 30). *Making family meals enjoyable*. Www.healthyfamiliesbc.ca.

https://www.healthyfamiliesbc.ca/home/articles/making-family-meals-enjoyable-preschool

Hyatte, A. (2020, January 26). *How to get your family excited about mealtime*. Whole Family Living. https://www.wholefamilyliving.com/get-your-family-excited-about-mealtime/

Jackson, J. (2021, November 10). *When your child feels most distant, seize the opportunity*. Connected Families. https://connectedfamilies.org/my-daughter-is-distant-from-me/

Karen. (2021, May 14). *9 reasons why you should read together as a family*. Markham Public Library. https://markhampubliclibrary.ca/blogs/post/9-reasons-why-you-should-read-together-as-a-family/

Keri. (2014, September 30). *5 criteria for selecting read-aloud books for children*. Year Round Homeschooling. https://www.yearroundhomeschooling.com/5-criteria-selecting-read-aloud-books-children/

Lee, K. (2019). *Projects children can do to help those in need*. Verywell Family.

https://www.verywellfamily.com/volunteer-ideas-for-kids-620308

Li, P. (2020, November 30). *Parent-Child relationship: How to strengthen it.* Parenting for Brain. https://www.parentingforbrain.com/close-parent-child-relationship/

M, K. (2021, November 12). *Parent-Child relationship: Why is it important and how to build it.* MomJunction. https://www.momjunction.com/articles/helpful-tips-to-strengthen-parent-child-bonding_0079667/#ParentChildRelationship3

Macquarrie, A. (2018, May 1). *The benefits of kids' DIY projects and how to find them.* Learning Liftoff. https://www.learningliftoff.com/benefits-of-kids-diy-projects/

Magana, L. C., Myers-Walls, J. A., & Love, D. (2013, October 23). *Different types of parent-child relationships.* At Health. https://athealth.com/topics/different-types-of-parent-child-relationships-3/

McLaughlin, C. (n.d.). *35 family game night ideas.* Www.signupgenius.com. Retrieved November 22, 2021, from https://www.signupgenius.com/home/family-game-night-ideas.cfm

Palm, M. (n.d.). *5 ways to teach kids the value of volunteering.* UrbanFamily. Retrieved November 21, 2021, from http://news.urbansitter.com/blog/5-ways-to-teach-kids-the-value-of-volunteering

Peterson, J. (2019, March 3). *The benefits of DIY projects for children.* Borncute.com. https://borncute.com/the-benefits-of-diy-projects-for-children/

Reading together as a family is FUN! (2018, January 23). Torontopubliclibrary.typepad.com. https://torontopubliclibrary.typepad.com/kids-books/2018/01/according-to-abc-life-literacy-just-fifteen-minutes-a-day-abc-life-literacy-canadas-activitiesto-read-or-do-a-learning-act.html

Swanson, M. (n.d.). *Is your teen pulling away? 7 ways you might be causing it.* Monicaswanson.com. Retrieved November 17, 2021, from https://monicaswanson.com/what-you-might-be-doing-to-push-your-teenager-away/

Tartakovsky, M. (2018, January 13). *5 habits that disconnect you from your kids.* Psych Central. https://psychcentral.com/lib/5-habits-that-disconnect-you-from-your-kids#1

Utter, J., Larson, N., Berge, J. M., Eisenberg, M. E., Fulkerson, J. A., & Neumark-Sztainer, D. (2018). Family meals among parents: Associations with nutritional, social and emotional wellbeing. *Preventive Medicine*, *113*, 7–12. https://doi.org/10.1016/j.ypmed.2018.05.006

Walton, K., Horton, N. J., Rifas-Shiman, S. L., Field, A. E., Austin, S. B., Haycraft, E., Breen, A., & Haines, J. (2018). Exploring the role of family functioning in the association between frequency of family dinners and dietary intake among adolescents and young adults. *JAMA Network Open*, *1*(7), e185217. https://doi.org/10.1001/jamanetworkopen.2018.5217

Winston, R., & Chicot, R. (2016). The importance of early bonding on the long-term mental health and resilience of children. *London Journal of Primary Care*, *8*(1), 12–14. https://doi.org/10.1080/17571472.2015.1133012

www.ingramcontent.com/pod-product-compliance
Lightning Source LLC
LaVergne TN
LVHW051018080826
845145LV00009B/2687

* 9 7 8 1 9 5 6 0 1 8 2 6 4 *